Coloring Books for Grownups

Wizard of Oz

VISIT TODAY
ILoveColoringBooksForAdults.com
TO WIN A SET OF PREMIUM COLORED PENCILS

Cover and page design by Cool Journals Studios - Copyright 2015

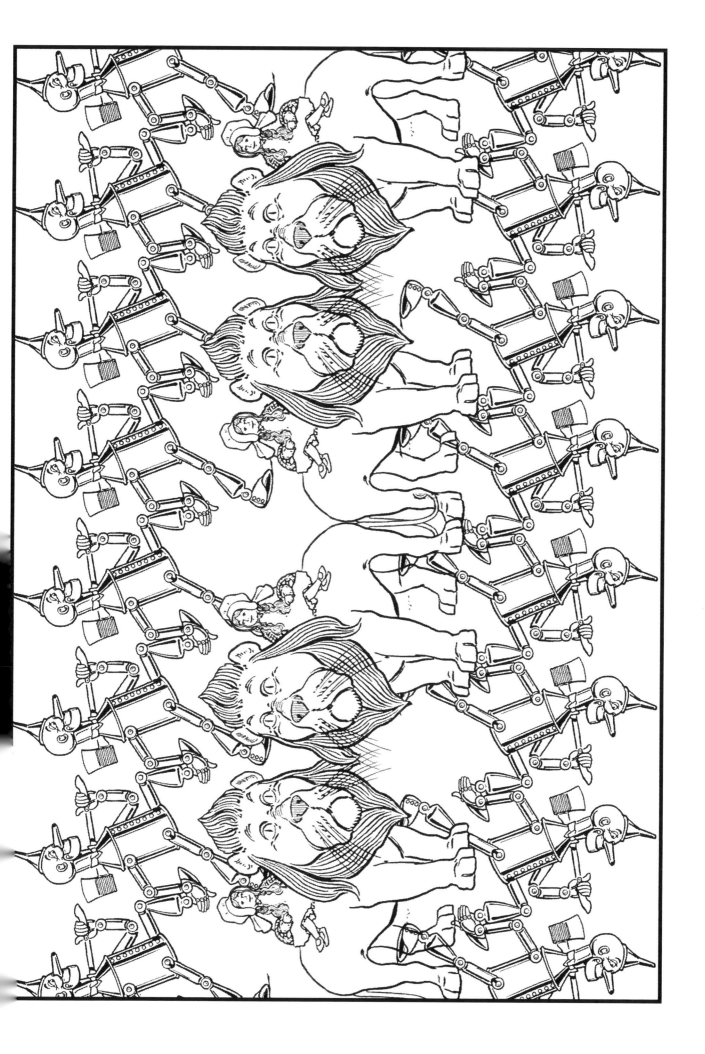

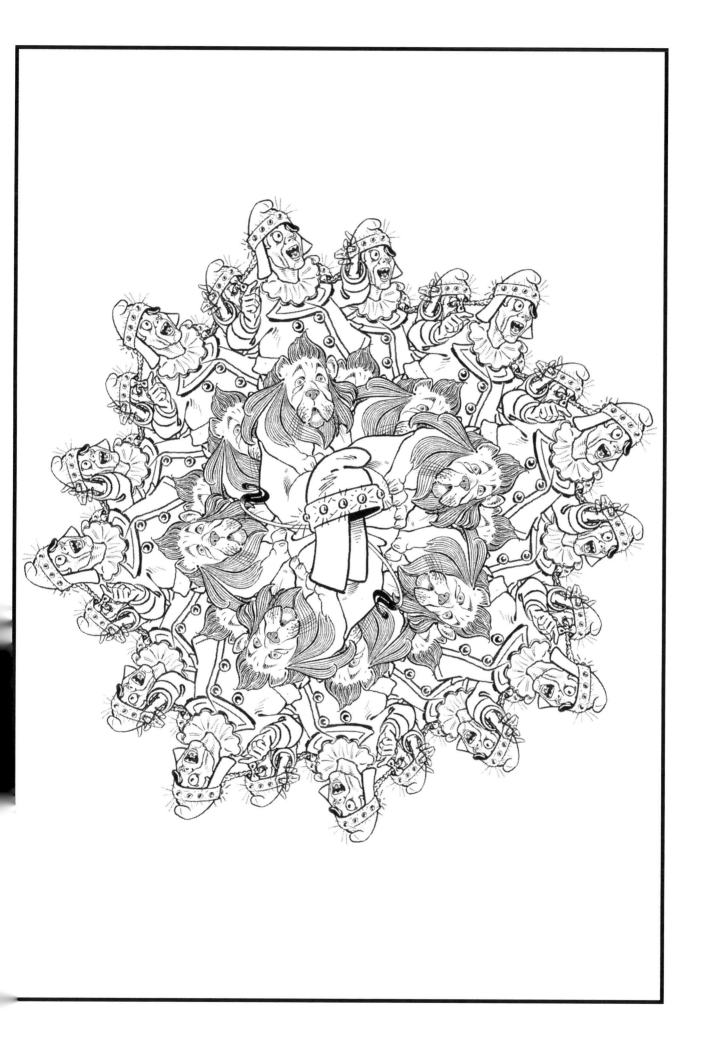

ALL YOU NEED
IS CONFIDENCE
IN YOURSELF

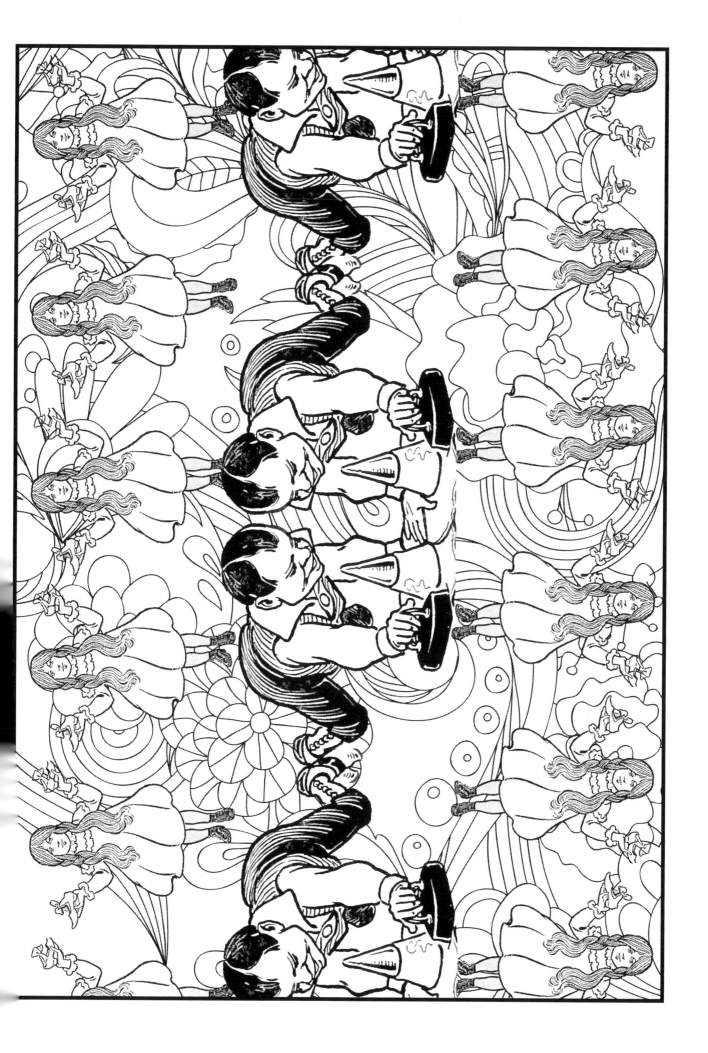

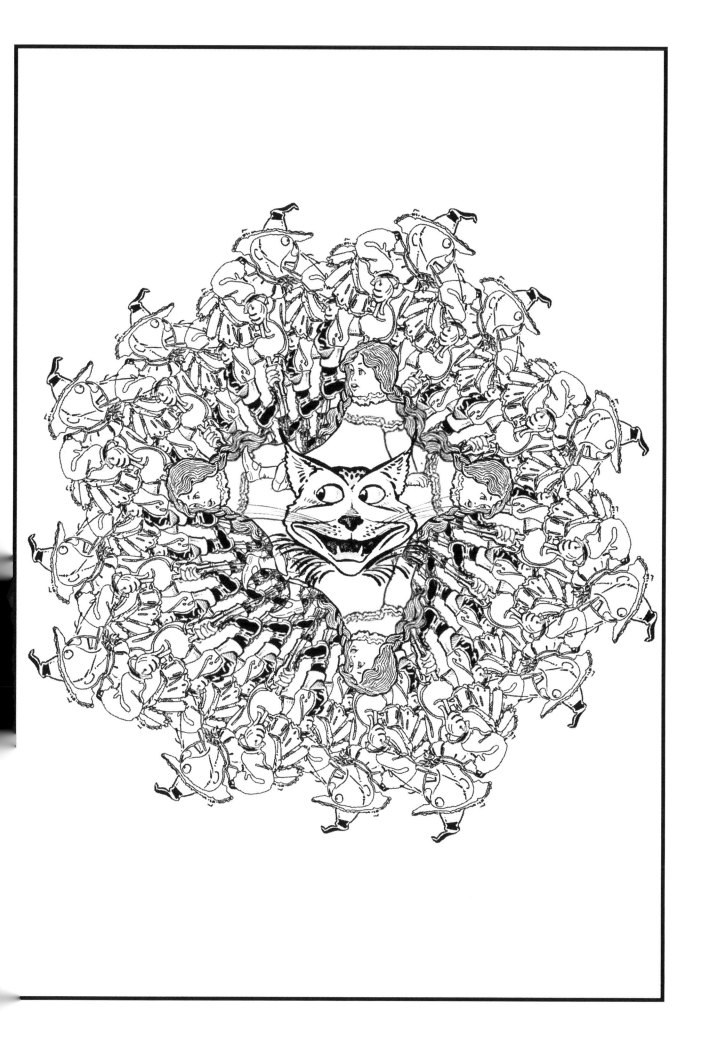

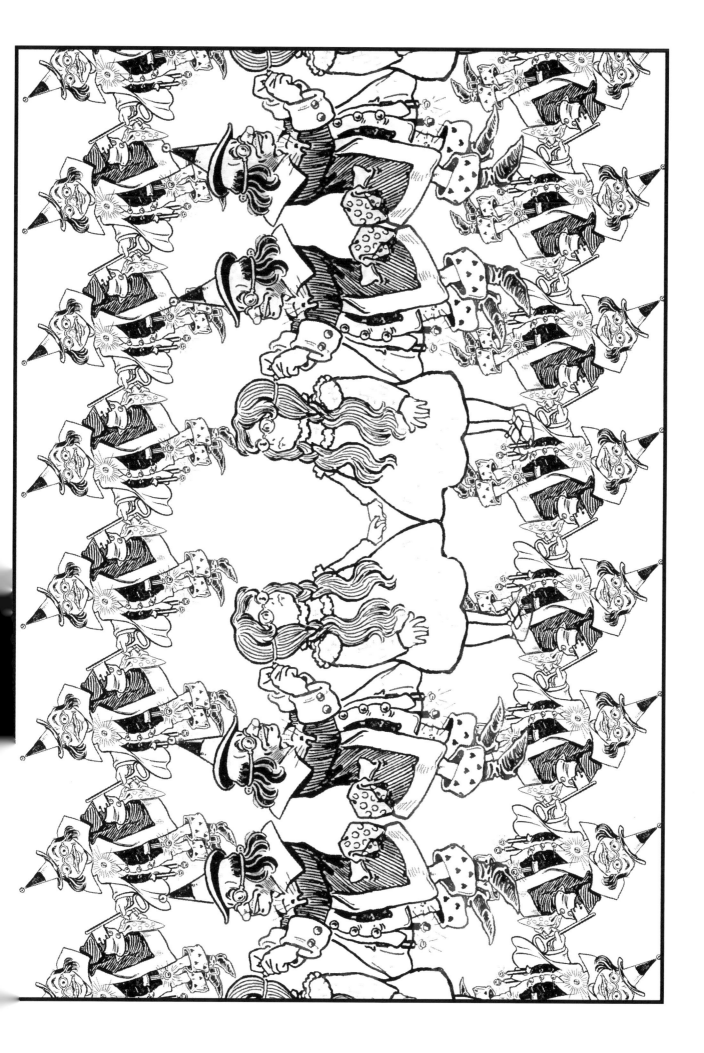

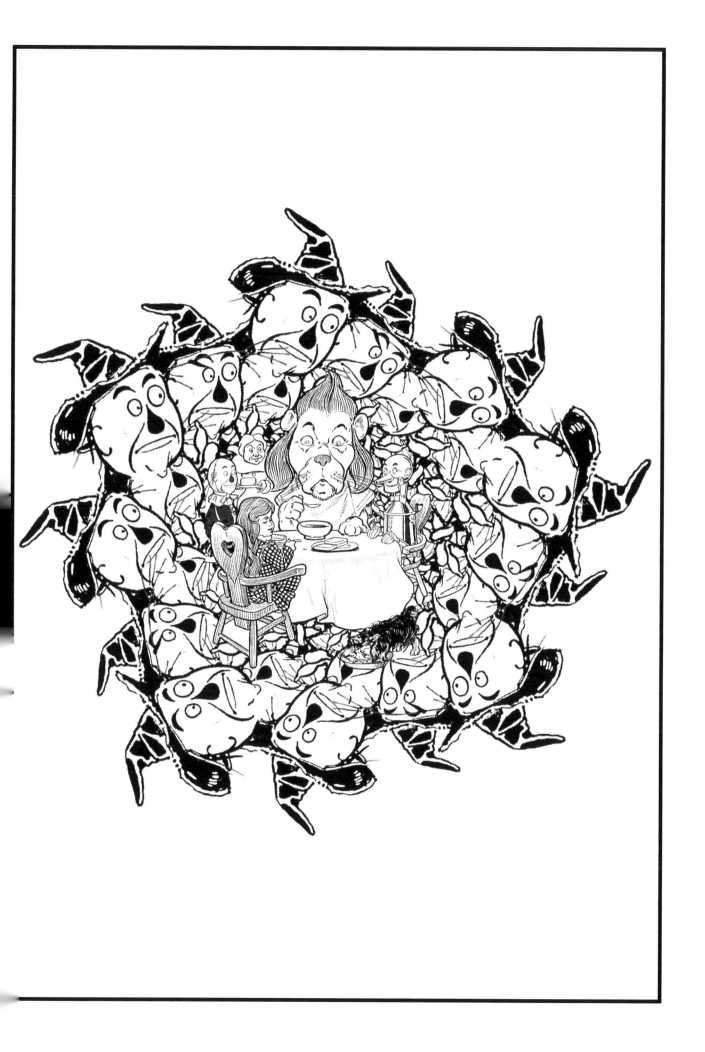

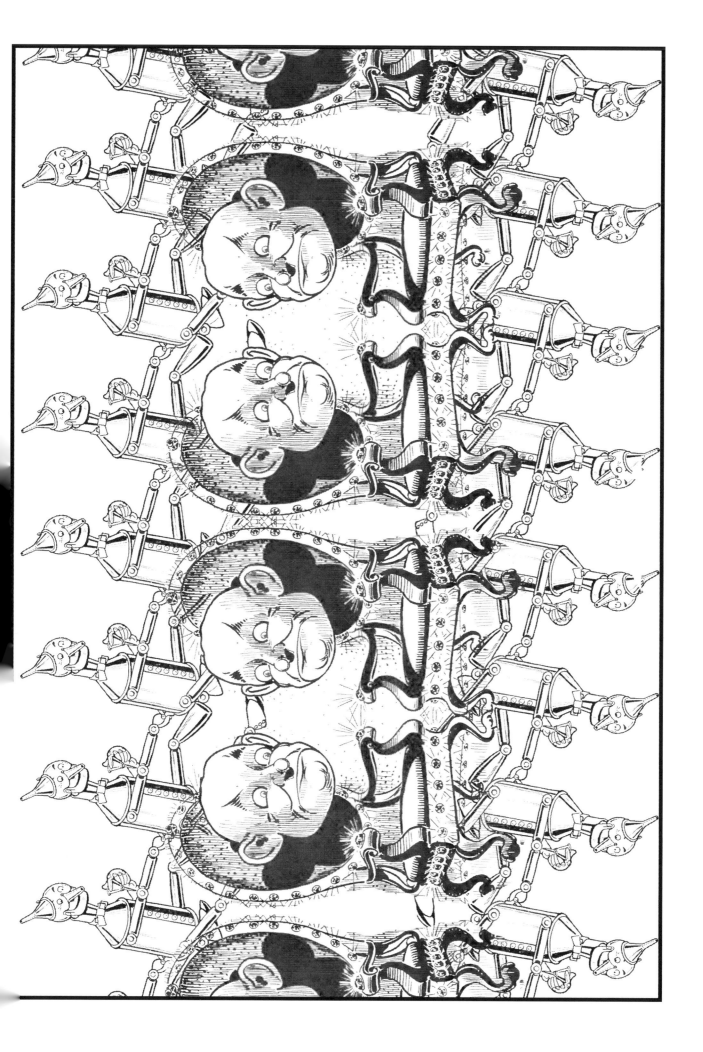

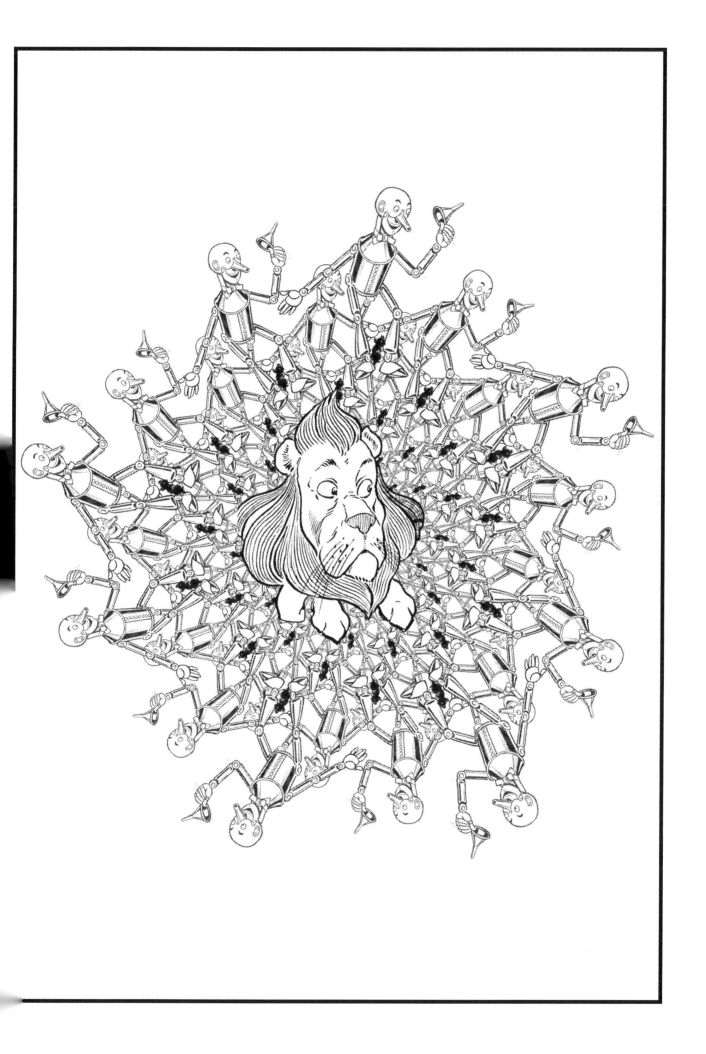

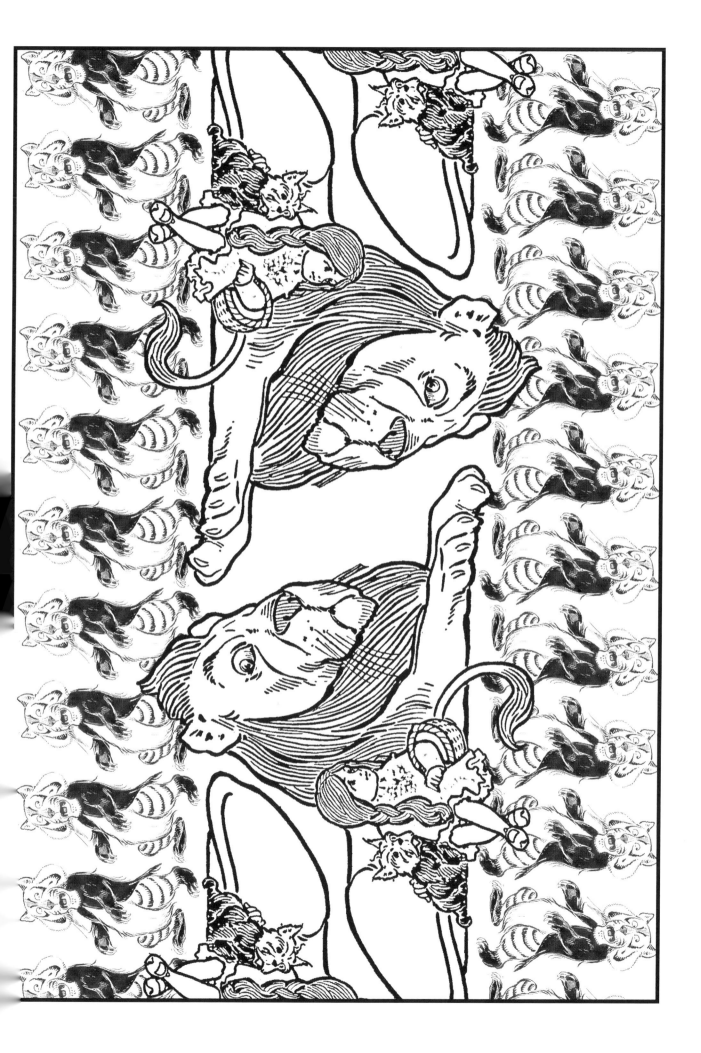

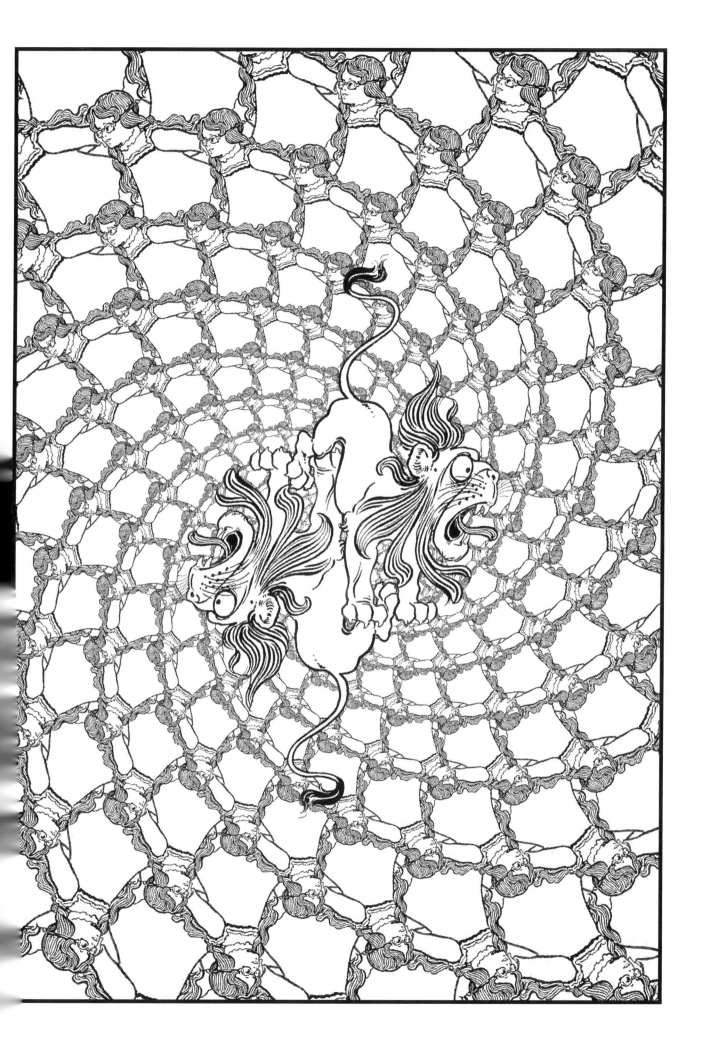

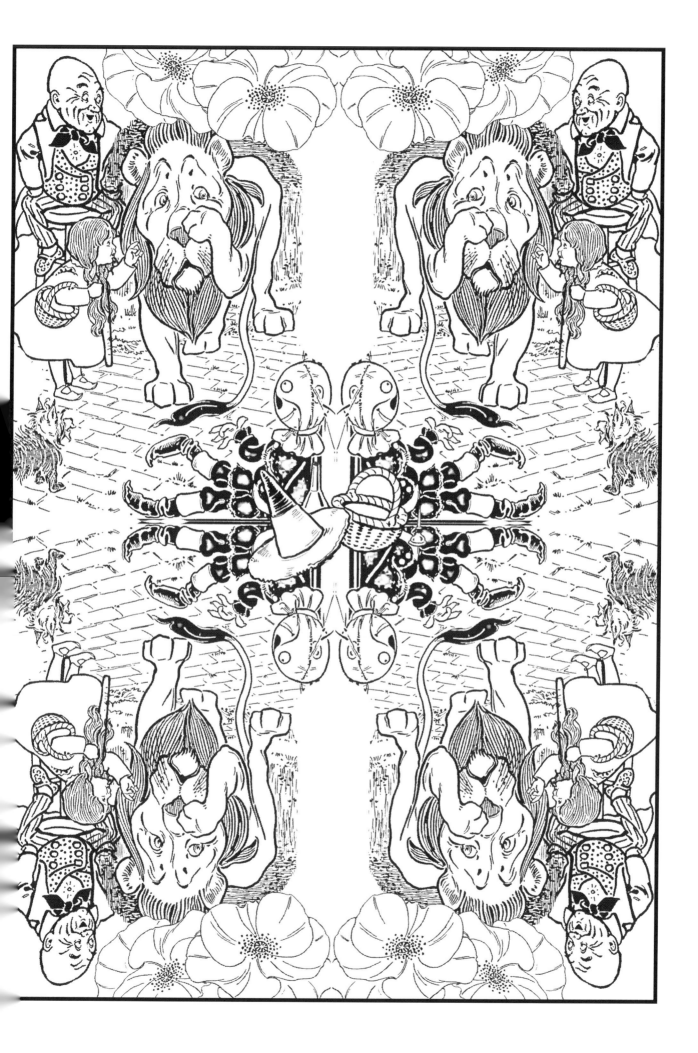

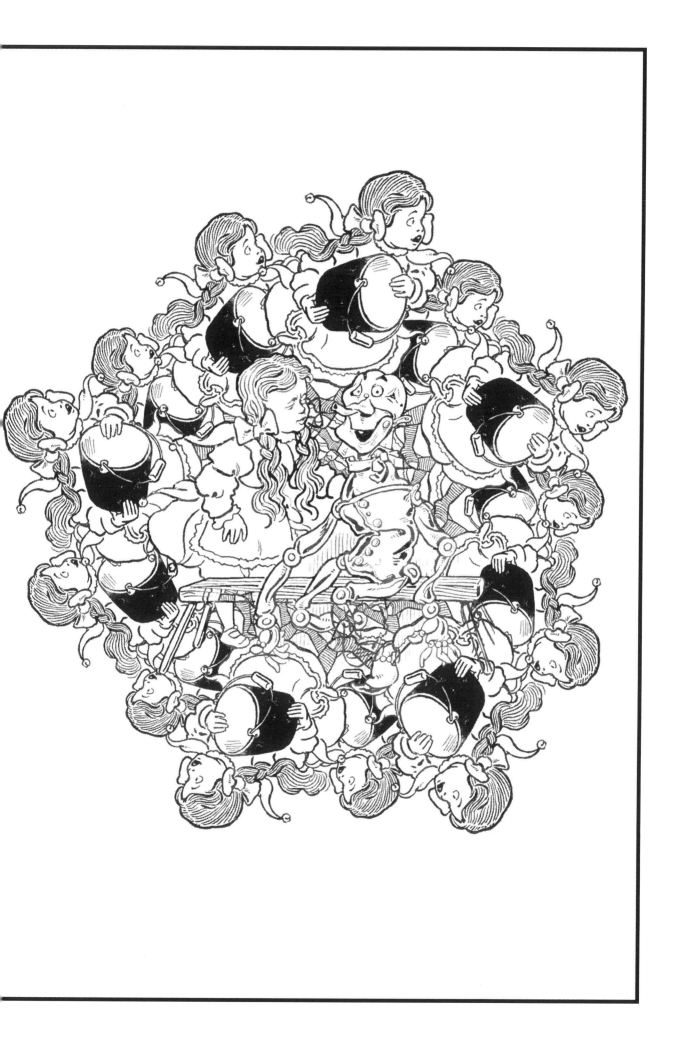

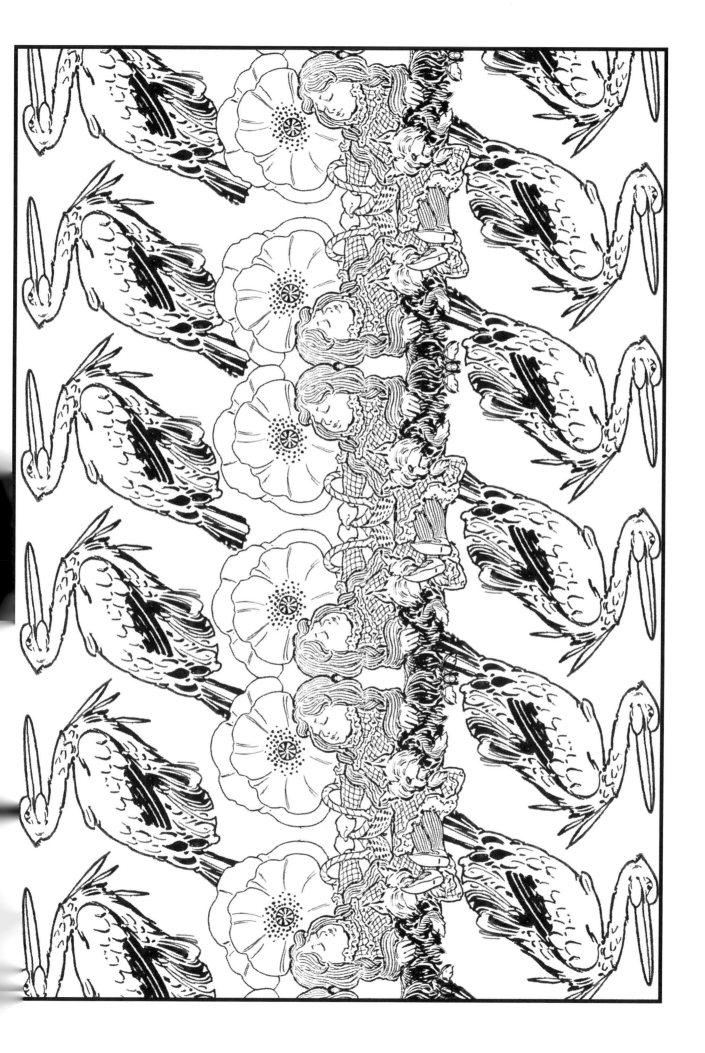

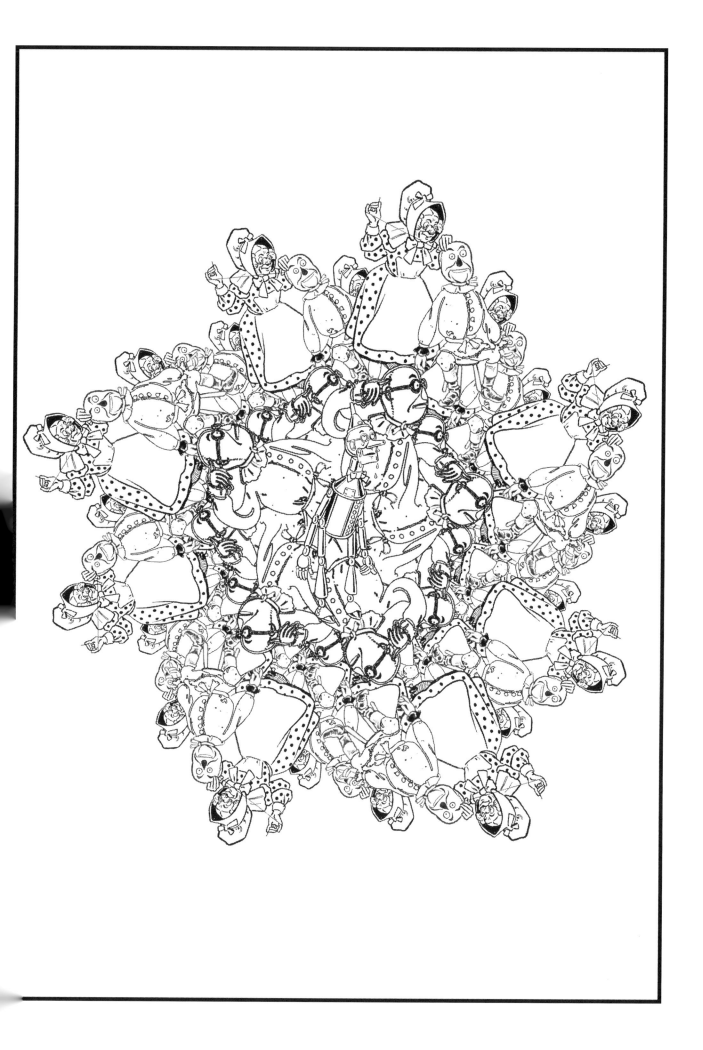

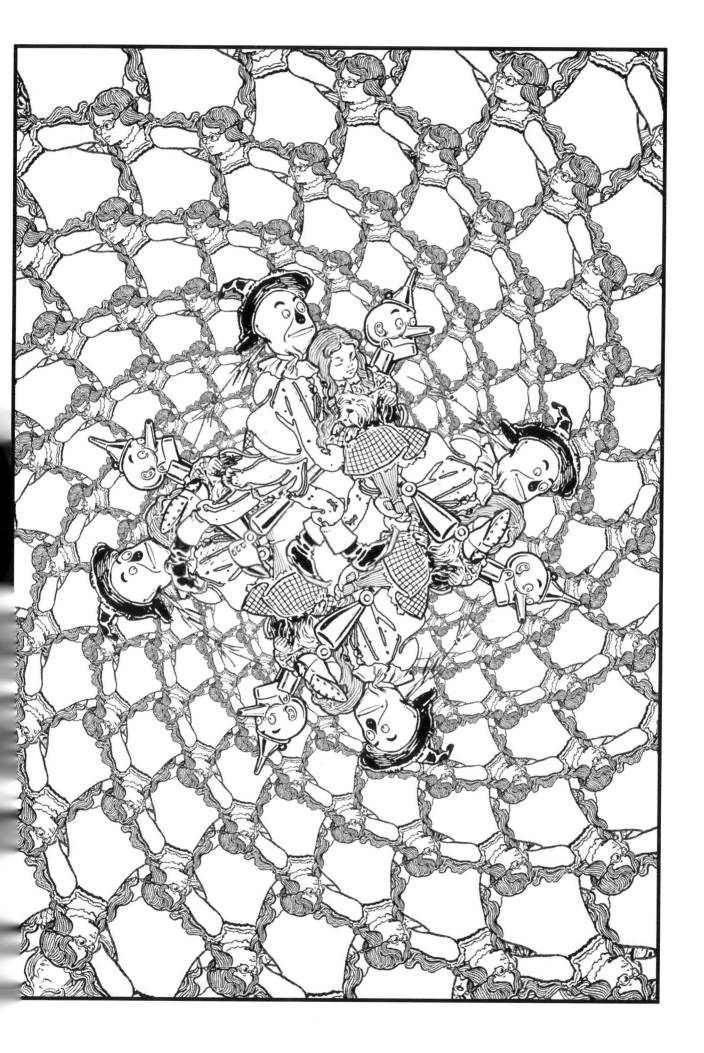

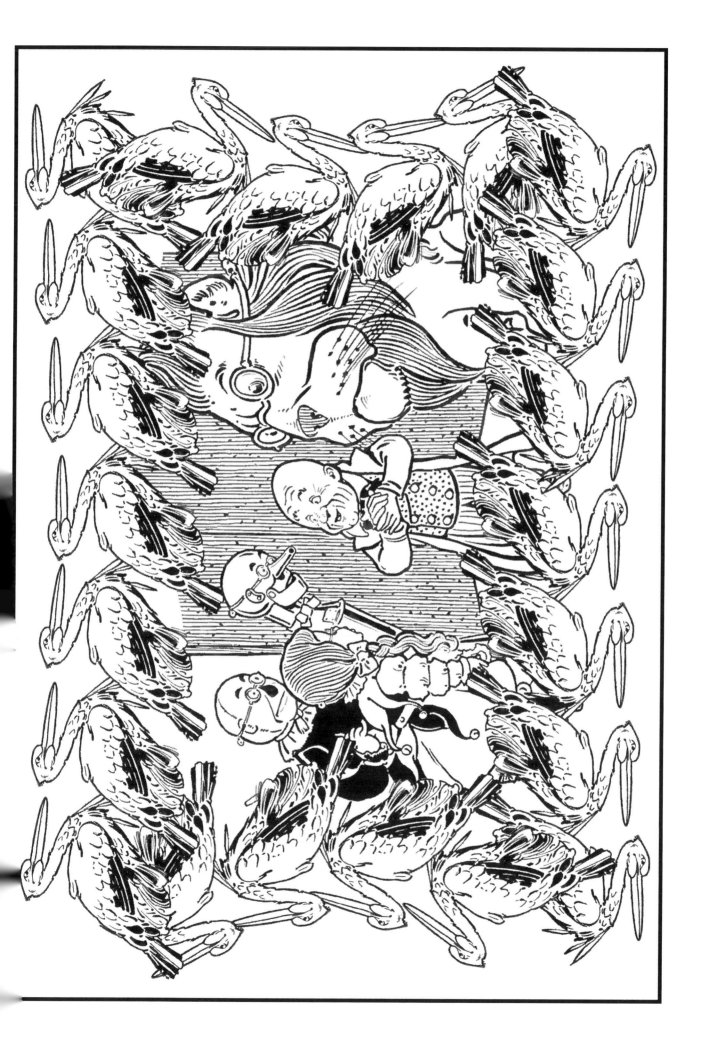

31318130R00059

Made in the USA
San Bernardino, CA
07 March 2016